The Love We Never Made

Text copyright © 2018 by Darryl Holiday Jr.

All rights reserved, including the right of reproduction in whole or in part in any form.

The text of this book is set in Garamond

Library of Congress Cataloging-in -Publication Data

Title by Darryl Holiday Jr.

ISBN: 978-0-692-10957-1

Visit tlwnm.com

Genre/ Categories the book could be placed under: 1. Poetry. 2. Romance.

Book Design by Nia Beasley

Editing by Kaci Diane Palmore

Manufactured in America

SCP 10 9 8 7 6 5 4 3 2 1

Table of Contents

Part One: Encounter   7
Dream   8
Tainted   9
Vibrations   10
Restless   11
Fall   12
Sense   13
Submit   14
Part Two: Passion   15
Again   16
Sunrise   17
Escape   18
Purpose   19
Soul   20
Dive   21
Influence   22
Belong   23
Waves   24
Scars   25

Part Three: Madness	26
Gluttony	27
Haven	28
Love Story	29
Heartbreak Station	30
Hindsight	31
Closer	32
Elevator Music	33
Love Letter	34
Cliff	35
Bottomless	36
Part Four: Relapse	37
Senseless	38
Nude	39
Paint	40
Peak	41
Flesh	42
Dark	43
Use me	44
Rainy Days	45
Raw	46
Night	47

Part Five: Denial 48
Addiction 49
Soul Ties 50
Abstract 51
Lost 52
Void 53
Shooting Star 54
Tomorrow 55
Full Circle 56
Masked 57
Pink Moscato 58
Part Six: Farewell 59
Nobody 60
Flashback 61
Exit 62
Raincheck 63
Recollection 64
Endless 65
Heat of the Moment 66
Cycle 67
Sunset 68
The Love We Never Made 69

Part One: Encounter

Dream

plagued by reality
pleasured by our dreams

we cringed at love
we welcomed heartache

we never knew what to do next
we just knew what we wanted to be

the beauty in the mystery
the ugliness of the unknown

escaping within each other
as long as we can

Tainted

So, the world managed to get its hands on you too,
sometimes I wonder what made you embrace the darkness,
but none of that matters anymore.
The way you smile leads me to believe that you like it better this way-
getting closer to your demons.
No...
you won't get to heaven this way-
but that's no longer your concern.
You just want to live.
The assets you have to offer,
you just want to give-
as long as you're satisfied in return.
Ignited by lust your fire burns.
Incapable of becoming who you once were,
you became just like me,
tainted.

Vibrations

I never fathomed how something so broken could be so beautiful.
She bore a scar on her lips from when love last kissed her.
I can hear the pain in her voice every time she speaks.
So broken that she can't be put together anymore,
Lost,
though she knows exactly what she's looking for.
Distraught,
though she smiles like she believes in second chances.
Her eyes glisten like city lights that encompass a million romances.
Somehow her smile makes the pain from love look worth it.
Maybe I'm just like her and I'm just afraid to show it on the surface.

Restless

The city never slept and neither did you.
Captivated by the beauty in your restless eyes,
as the bright lights became our path's guide
it no longer mattered where we went as long as I was with you.
We owned the world as we drifted through the packed streets.
Everyone was standing like mannequins and I felt like we were the
only ones who existed.
When you smiled I saw it in slow motion like time took a while
just so the moment would not too soon pass me by.
If love feels like this I never want it to leave.
Your lips touched mine and I've never tasted anything so sweet.
Tears of joy consoled my sight for what I was about to see.
People started moving again and before I could react you were gone,
and I was left alone in the city that refuses to sleep.

Fall

Who knew tears of joy could hurt just as much,
resisting our desires,
pulsed by spiritual vibrations,
avoiding what inevitably accompanies them.

Physical sensations displaying their craftiness of mending what's broken,
though we would never admit it to be,
a hopeless place we cannot stay,
a way away from the world.

Admirably embracing the grains of sand that time allows us to grasp,
mesmerized by the feeling,
numbed by the pain,
as it slowly slips through our fingers.

A distant sight that our eyes yearn to see each day,
heights we may never reach,
so, it is okay,
if we fall.

Sense

Uncapped emotions overflow as our temperatures reach their boiling points and the only parts of our bodies that have interlocked are our eyes.
I press my face against yours just to feel the softness of your skin, wanting the feeling to never leave.
Our lips finally meet, and we taste each other for the first time.
Taking deep breaths while we kiss as if to help each other breathe.
I bite your bottom lip just to make sure the pleasure and pain you feel is in their correct tandem.
You open the doors to your temple and give in to me
as we harmonize like symphonies as our desires clash.
Our bodies speak languages that only they understand
as we are fascinated by their fluency in awe.
Captivated by murmured words that only hold truth during these moments.
Moments we often revisit,
just to hear them again.

Submit

I wonder if temptations say the same things to you.
We crave predicaments that we dare not to say to one another.
However,
no words need to be spoken for we both know exactly why we are here.
The rain did us a favor by shedding its tears tonight,
providing us with tempo as our cries crescendo while we perform on natures stage.
Exhale,
and breathe into me as if you've never lived before this moment,
while I tunnel deeply inside of you as if to plant a seed of life at your core.
You press your forehead against mine and we lock eyes telepathically speaking,
as all our emotions perspire through our skin we continue on.
We mix emotions,
hoping
we never
submit.

Part Two: Passion

Again

the sun goes down
i can feel the vibrations in the air
your body's calling me
we move to the beat of the night
blinded by passion
possessed by temptation
enjoying every moment
of exactly where we wish to be
within each other
between these sheets
we dare not speak
nor tell a soul
of these secrets we keep
every night we meet
when the sun goes down
and every night we love
like it's our first time

Sunrise

Careful not to wake you,
I gently kiss your forehead good morning.
Breakfast in bed and you're all that's on the menu.
Your fruit glistens with its succulent sap and it tastes exactly like paradise.
I slowly caress your inner thighs with my tongue.
Just enough to put your sensations on edge.
You then let out a deep moan.
Which is overpowered by your hands fiercely clenching the bed.
I speak to you in tongues.
You rub your hands on my head as you feel every syllable heard.
Tranquilized,
as if I touched your soul with the tip of my tongue.
The sun's rays begin to sneak in between the blinds just as soon as you climax.
Your breathing hastens but I continue to take my time,
so you can experience every millisecond this moment has to offer,
as you watch the sunrise.

Escape

Somehow,
we travel through time.
She takes me to a place where I feel like I belong-
a place where I know I can't stay long.
So old school,
a timeless heart with a tempo that I'd like to get old to,
never allowing anything the ability to control you.
I admire that.
No,
I adore you.
We ended up on the same path.
Together we walked, we ran, we fell, and we laughed.
Somehow,
we traveled through time.
Even though forever never lasts,
you will always be
my escape.

Purpose

I can't stop thinking about you.
Infatuated with seemingly unattainable thoughts of simplicity
where journeys traveled don't decide what the future may hold.
The longevity sustained by the pain has numbed your tongue from talks of freedom
but your eyes refuse to refrain from telling the story.
Who knew an alleged villain could possibly become your hero?
Who knew that the forbidden fruit would fall ever so close to you?
Eve...
let me be your Adam and together let's break free of the worlds status quo.
Allow me to show you something new,
to motivate you to adventure to places that alone you would never go,
to provide emotional healing and reverse this feeling you currently loathe.
Even through the storm there's one thing I'll always firmly believe...
There are a million reasons why we shouldn't-
but there's a million and one
why it's meant to be.

Soul

love
I must confess
that these pleasures of the flesh have started to sink within my soul

I undress you with my eyes
slowly removing your garments
while grazing your body with my fingertips
just enough to heighten your senses
I rub my face against yours
passionately kiss you from cheek to cheek
biting your bottom lip
pulling just hard enough for you to know who it belongs to,
I continue to explore you
Sliding my tongue from your lips
down your neck
as I speak sweet nothings to your skin,
I cover your areolas
with my tongue
showing your breasts
all the attention they've ever wanted
I kiss down your chest
making my way to your waist
seeking to speak to the bud of your flower
without removing the petals just to tease you a little while longer
I remove the last of your leaves
and devour your succulent nectar
consuming all your precious nutrition

you hold me under so long that I dive inside
stroking through your ocean searching for your hidden treasure
tunneling to your core reaching for your epicenter

love
I must confess
I want your soul

Dive

We're here again,
Falling in love as we fall into each other,
But we dare not utter those words,
Even if within this very moment we truly mean them,
This is everything we ever wanted,
Everything we could never have,
So we grasp each other,
As if we could actually never let go.

Influence

As we journey under the influence
we distance ourselves from coincidence
and become lost within the moment.
Neither of us should be here
and the thought of it makes us embrace every second even more.
Senses heightened.
Blurred likeness.
This euphoria has become my utopia
and you are the very high I've been searching for.
Love me now.
Love me forever.
And when we part never love me again.

Belong

Passionate thoughts become reality
as our silence is broken by our bodies speaking the same language.
You ask how we ended up here
knowing that you never want to go back.
Receive me, arch your back and grant me access to your assets
assets that no one else could fully handle.

Let me, journey inside you
questing to provide you everything you ever asked for.
Believe me, I plan to give you all you need
until you can't take anymore.
Until you
belong
to me.

Waves

unwarranted passion
whose fashions are only told by time.
raw emotions
that inflict just as much pain as they do satisfaction.
invisible scars
that mark our hearts each time our bodies collide.
utter silence
is what makes it so beautiful.
please don't
lose sight of that.

Scars

I know you're trying to forget.
It's just that I can't help but see the beauty in the scars you try so hard to hide.
It may sound peculiar, but I can tell that love once loved you too.
A familiar look in your eyes solidifies that pain does not pity the fool.
I know you're not hiding as much from the world as you are from you.
Who am I to ask you to travel down this forsaken road again?

I know you're trying to forget.
You have allowed these scars that have populated your skin
to sink within the walls of your battered heart.
It seems that the addition of insult to injury is an understatement.
I'm sorry…

I know you're trying to forget.
I just want you to let me save you from you,
show you that as much as it can hurt love can also heal.
Unveil my disguise and discover that I have scars too.
I'm asking you to travel down this road with me.
So I can forget too.

Part Three:

Madness

Gluttony

You remind me of someone that I know wants to forget me.
It's a feeling so familiar.
So... tempting.
I wonder at what moment I was consumed by my own appetite.
I wonder if I'll feel the same way after you come.
And... go.
I've realized that I ran out of love long ago.
Now I have just enough lust to stay afloat.

Haven

You wear your hurt on your sleeve exactly where your heart used to be.
Your voice trembles with pain even though you try to hide it with adamant projection.
Constantly, you embrace this wall that you've created for protection... from yourself.
Honestly,
I understand you more than you'd care to believe.
So much so, that I'd even let you wrongfully place the blame on me.
I allow you to slowly take out all your pain on me,
just long enough for you to see,
that I too,
once had to save myself
from me.

Love Story

We stuck stickers to street poles marking our ventures for the world to see.
At bus stops waiting, we had conversations of fantasies we wish could really be.
She had a smile so serene, she could show happiness how happy it could actually be.
Pinching pennies out of her pockets, she tried to afford more worldly sights for us to see.
It wasn't until I saw her smile fade that I realized how much I loved her.
So I began to do things that I'm not proud of because I knew we desperately needed the money.
I think that's why I can't look her in her eyes anymore.
She left me alone to see the world.
She followed the dreams she had since she was a little girl.
I always wonder what could have been if it was the two of us together in the end.
Now I'm at this bus stop waiting with nowhere to go.
Wishing this dreamt up reality will someday let me go.

Heartbreak Station

The beautiful thing about denial is the fact that you do believe yourself.
I wonder if I asked you how you ended up here if you'd tell me the truth.
I'm patiently waiting at this abandoned station refusing to embark on another route.
Maybe you're supposed to be joined by someone else and that's why you haven't moved.
But every train has a schedule and even this one will be leaving soon.
Who am I to judge because I'm here along with you.
The difference is that I'm here by choice and I don't have nearly as many bags as you.
When I try to help you carry them on the train you say that you're okay.
Your lips tell me lies that your eyes would never fathom to say.
I wonder if you know that you won't get far by taking those bags with you.
I fear that you're aware that this is the same train that brought you here.
How naive of me to believe that you ever wanted to leave Heartbreak Station.

Hindsight

Sometimes I take the long way home just to see the city skyline
so your voice can cloud my mind
about your dreams and things you saw that other people just couldn't.
See, I was never as optimistic as you
but at times I too wished your perception was indeed reality.
The way your eyes gleamed could outshine the city's lights on any
given night.
No attractions were nearly as attractive as you,
but I'd be a fool to allow one to assume that the most beautiful part
of you had anything to do with your skin's surface.
You just had so much soul...
your aura emitted positivity, warmth, and glow.
You made me feel at home, even when I was on the road.
That's why I'm always taking the long way home.

Closer

I just hope that sometimes you smile when you think of me.
We're trapped in times,
that time wouldn't let us hold in our hands for too long.
I'm holding on to these moments closer than I ever held you.
Our memories are trapped in my mind, I couldn't release them even if I wanted to.
In hindsight I realize that we never loved,
even though we tried so hard,
even though it felt so good.
So many times we should have let go.
Although we refused,
we both knew we should.
I just want to know,
is it wrong for me to wonder,
is it wrong for me to want to...
do it again.

Elevator Music

Devils were disguised as angels but they're tired of hiding their horns now,
Your demons are upset because they have to let you go now,
The world has stopped revolving because it has to let you grow now,
You rose from concrete, but you're armored with thorns now,
The darkness of closed doors eclipses your sun now,
It's a shame that the pain has you numb now,
I realized that thoughts of you are all I have now,
The only images I ever wish to see,
The only tone I ever wish to hear,
I'm afraid our door has closed,
I'm afraid we'll never escape from here.

Love Letter

I wonder what it would feel like to forget you,
to lose sight of those eyes that were once only for me.
You used to be the heartbeat to keep me alive,
now you cause my heart to skip beats in my dreams.

I wonder what it would feel like to forget you,
because I feel the same passion in your cold stare that I did in your warm embrace.
I just hope that you hate me as much as you loved me,
and if we had the opportunity to do it all again that you would.

I wonder what it would feel like to forget you,
to be able to visit venues of memories without that inner trembling.
so I can once again love without my heart automatically fending,
to stop avoiding any caring hands that are truthfully lending,
themselves to me.

I wonder what it would feel like to forget you,
to forget that goodnight kiss that helped me sleep,
to forget how you had my back when the world turned on me,
to forget how you opened my eyes towards my goals
when the darkness made it hard to see.

I wonder what it would feel like to forget you.
Sometimes I wonder what it would feel like to love you again.
The same way I wonder where we would be right now,
if you were still here.

Cliff

Standing here I've realized this,
I don't think I can ever love someone the way that I loved you.
Flashbacks of you are memories more beautiful than any scenic view.
I'm seeing similarities in all current attractions because my eyes still hold on to you,
Completely negligent I ignored that every high has a contrasting low too,
I just wish I could have held on to my heart,
when I lost you.

Bottomless

Long gone but I can't let go.
I found bliss in the dark abyss by holding on to this feeling.
Comforted myself with the warmth from thoughts of what it's like to hold you.
Always awakened by the cold reality of you no longer here beside me.
I cling to the walls of my heart as if they were constructed from pieces of you,
There are times that I hear your voice echo in my head,
calling for me...
Memories feel so real.
It still feels like I'm falling for you.
Love,
I'd fall for you forever.
I just don't want to feel the bottom.

Part Four: Relapse

Senseless

All I heard was a knock at the door,
and there you were standing with a raincoat.
But, it wasn't raining...
I began to kiss your neck
and every sound in the world was cancelled out by your deep breaths.
I began to pull your hair back and choke you as I proceeded to bite your bottom lip because I didn't want to hear anything.
I just wanted to feel you...
You raised your right leg and grazed my hip as my hand gripped and began to part the sea between your inner thighs.
I turned you around and pressed your body against the door.
The contact caused your raincoat to drop to the floor.
I removed my shirt and started to tie your hands behind your back.
I've been waiting for you to bring your body to me and I don't want you to go anywhere.
You slowly arched your back so I could slip inside of you.
I could feel sensations dripping off of you onto me.
Hours passed as our bodies tangled willingly.
As feelings came,
they soon decided to leave,
until we,
laid there,
senseless.

Nude

There she is lying still with nothing on,
vibrantly posing for me while I sit in front of this canvas.
She's patiently waiting to be drawn,
but her curves strike my nerves and I can't stand it.
I want to capture her soul with my brush flow and be her bandit.
It's the way her eyes glow; they won't let me go.
I make her shadows show, as my brush goes to and fro,
because the unique way her tone shades I know nobody knows.
The beautiful scenes to which her curves lead I know nobody goes.
She's here for me,
allowing me to be her sailor, allowing me to map her sea.
It's intimacy,
my brush doing her body favors,
with every thrust the more I lust her layers.
Her luscious skin more tempting than sin,
makes every ounce of my being cringe.
Like a cheetah untamed she runs my mind insane,
I wonder what she's thinking.
Maybe she thinks of me.
Maybe she's thinking of the canvas,
and the reflection she soon shall see.
Maybe she knows I planned this.
Maybe now she'll only bring her body to me,
because once she's trapped in this canvas,
only my brush can set her free.

Paint

I miss seeing you naked.
Creating bursts of colors and emotions as I dipped my paintbrush in your unique potion.
It's amazing the artwork we produced
when my paintbrush used to profusely stroke against your canvas.
Scratches, teardrops, handprints...
beautiful madness.
We made senseless love from every angle in tandem,
unintentional inspirations led to habitual sensations.
We mentally framed our finished pieces just to see if we could reach that peak again,
masterpieces we could never again recreate.
You inspired me like no other,
when I loved you.

Peak

embark on this journey with me
as I help you discover who you really are
tell me everything about you
but I don't want you to say a word
let me graze your stripes and your curves with my fingertips
as I learn your body's language
allow me to court you as I slowly escort you towards your peak
you sink your nails into my skin
and I reciprocate the pressure while embracing your thighs
I devour my three-course meal while staring in your eyes
I slide up until we're at eye-level
I slide in until your breaths thin
you then lose all wind and like Adam and Eve
at the ribs we're connected again,
sights set on cloud 9 as we complete our ascension
please hold on
and don't let go

Flesh

the despise in your eyes has made its way to the windows of my soul
you want to inflict pain on me while enjoying every minute of it
and I wish to experience every ounce of emotion you have left to offer
you hate me...but not enough
the reminiscent pleasures I endowed upon your flesh still control your soul
it drives you...empowers you even
just enough to make your way back to me
memories meddle with current moments monumentally clouding your judgement
leaving you to crave something deeper than the skin
something of more substance
but here you are
looking for something you will never find
in the dark

Dark

dark rooms lit by old flames
but I can't seem to feel the warmth anymore
as the flame flickers
I wonder if it's the only thing that time has gotten the best of
or if I just fail to realize the rest of the situation at hand
it has to be cold in here all by yourself
I must say that I know the pain of taming the flame by oneself
all too well...
speechless with so much to say
I wish I understood this message you're trying to convey
trying to light the way in order to make me stay
but it's too late
extinguish the flame
and let us enjoy the dark
this moment we're no longer apart
before that's gone too

Use me

we could never belong to each other
yet our eyes reflect visions of decisions we both yearn to make
we bare untamed curiosity of primitive animosity
yet we crave a combined emotional, physical, and spiritual state
let me take you where you've never been
yet always wanted to go
trust me
if you don't know I can teach you
sensations from the building anticipation
cause the slightest touch to feel new
part of us wants this moment to come
but have no desire for tensions foreplay to come to an end
even though we will never belong to each other
we can always pretend
even if it's just for a moment

Rainy Days

the rain steadily knocks against the bedroom windows
curious to know what we do between the sheets
our lips passionately touch
and I can feel your breath slowly leave you
as I journey to your soul
we moan in each other's mouths
just so the rain won't know of the things we say
we switch positions without ever letting go of each other
grasping every moment every ounce we had to offer
the rain steadily knocked against the bedroom windows
curious to know what we do between the sheets
the rain knocked all night
and so did we

Raw

we fuck
like we've known each other for a lifetime
chest to chest
breath for breath
we connect like we're each other's lifelines
lost in the moment
looking for love in a place where it could never survive
even if that's what we wanted
but we hold on to that feeling
like we hold on to each other
desperately attempting
to never let go

Night

Rapid flashbacks of the love we've made stir your soul.
We searched for substance in temporary emotions.
Hoping that they'd stay around long enough for you to grab hold.
Once possessed into action by the passion,
now you've succumbed to hate and allowed it to consume you.
Love,
don't let the reemergence of the butterflies confuse you.
Hate me,
hate me more than you ever could have possibly loved me.
Hate me like you'll never have the chance to hate me again.
It's all fine with me,
as long as you remember how good it felt to do so.

Part Five: Denial

Addiction

You're no good, but you complete me.
Wondering if I willingly submit to you or you simply defeat me.
Either way I give in,
to the unsurmountable pleasure even at the cost of someone else's pain.
It's a shame how I've become so numb to it now.
Unconsciously, I go through the motions,
hoping that someday something will change
while enjoying every moment trapped in this loop of insanity.
I have plans to one day be over you the same way you hover over me,
refusing to let go
even though
at this point it's not clear who has the hold on whom.
Truth is,
I don't want to let you go.

Soul Ties

love
there's not much left inside you
inside you
wondering who I am
looking for love in the all the wrong places until lust crept in
then you realized love isn't what you've been looking for at all
at least that's not what you found
or maybe at one point it was but the timing was wrong
now there's been so much damage
you can't manage to remember who you were before it all
so many links to the chain that has now laid claim on your soul
enjoying your domain just as much as the desire to let the scenery go
once and for all
questing to please you as I once journeyed to please myself
knowing that my soul is tied
and there's not enough space for anyone else

Abstract

Bright colors become darker over time
like withered flowers without sunlight,
but there's a hint of beauty in apparent pain.
Fragmented lines or maybe broken shards
of a fragile heart you once held
that now only your eyes can muster to grasp.
Passion ties the loose ends back together
though they are far apart.
Strokes of emotions-
wild but precise
as if this moment was expected from the very beginning
and this image was meant just for you.
Blending colors like raw emotion
that show signs of distortion
as if real tears hit portions of this piece.
Wondering who feels more pain?
The muse.
Or me.

Lost

Every time the lights shut off it gets a little darker.
What was once a rush, has now become a must and has lost its luster.
It's to the point where you can't even see who you're with anymore.
No introductions,
just the sound of shed garments hitting the floor
and contraceptives finally being found inside the bedside drawer.
Slow kisses on the lips that lack passion,
a mind drifting away,
wondering how you got here and what happened,
To Lucius you might as well have sold your soul.
Love,
will the darkness ever let you go?

Void

I wonder if we ever look at the stars at the same time,
the same way we once shared visions of a future together.
I guess I'm not over you after all,
but I don't think anything will change even if I do admit that.
What do you do with a void that can't be filled?
A void that stretches as far as the night sky...
I'd assume that you'd admire its everlasting beauty,
and you'd reminisce on the good times.

Shooting Star

For a while I thought someone like you didn't exist.
Maybe it's because you remind me of something I never had.
Or someone that I miss.
But this spark,
this flash.
I've never seen anything like this.
You're like a shooting star.
So I'll close my eyes and make a wish.
You're smile lingers around me even when you leave.
Your voice is softer than the wind when it rustles through the trees.
Why me?
Why'd I stop and window shop for something that won't be?
My stomachs' butterflies are tantalized and want to be set free,
but this spark.
This flash that I see,
it's not for me.
Why make a wish that probably won't be?
Maybe instead of wishing I'll dream.
So things won't be as hopeless as they seem.
And I'll see that shooting star once more.
And I'll never again feel like I felt before.

Tomorrow

I loved you like there was no tomorrow.
So when tomorrow finally came I had no clue what to do.
Seconds became days.
Which seemed like centuries.
Without you.
So empty.
So full of pain.
I embrace every ounce of emotion I have left.
Because it reminds me of you.
Every second.
Of everyday.

Full Circle

Baggage you excessively filled with bad habits,
so much pain from the strain.
Now the only thought your mind cares to maintain
is that your surroundings are all too familiar.
The question is no longer how did I get here,
it's why am I still here, and how the hell have I gotten so comfortable.
It's to the point where there is an amusing pleasure gained from the pain.
Occasionally, you contemplate if you deserve it
and if karma has led you right down the wrong path on purpose.
But it's not her fault at all.
It's because of you.
You're in new situations with the same decisions
accompanied by a mended heart with the same sharp ridges.
Naively handing out love as a double-edged sword
and wondering why it hurts you too.
Nostalgically entranced by the scenery
your eyes have now lost the desire to leave.
Maybe you belong here,
maybe now you're just in too deep.
Maybe you're back in the same place you started
and you just had to be on the other side of the same circle to see.

Masked

Disguised as the very image you think she wants to see,
Wondering how long undercover you plan to be,
Falsifying emotions to fulfill your own pleasures,
Fooling yourself hoping you'd one day forget her,
Cowering and concealed hiding what's real,

One day you're going to want to be you again.
Unless...
You've already forgotten who you are.

Pink Moscato

Pink Moscato,
I wish I could be you,
The way she drowns her emotions in your tonic potion,
I wish I could be her remedy too,
I wonder if the act of lusting to love is still considered a sin,
Lights dimmed,
Lipstick stained on the rim,
Clouds the regrets of past decisions,
Of someone who is now only referred to as "him,"
Pink Moscato,
Cooled by constant teardrops,
Contaminated by a mix of mascara and heartbreak,
I wish I could take her from you,
I wish she'd never drink you again,
But we both know that will never happen,
I may never see her again,
We both know that the only time she needs you,
Is when she's been left alone.

Part Six: Farewell

Nobody

I guess I still love you,
Cause I can't love nobody,
Searching for love in their bodies,
But I just feel emptied by it,
I think I still love you,
Cause I can't love nobody,
Cupid's arrow proves me hollow,
Just a vessel drowned in sorrow,
I hope I still love you,
Cause I can't love nobody,
Tears dress her body,
But I'm not that affected by it,
I know I still love you,
Cause I can't love nobody,
But at the same time,
I know I can't love you,
Cause I can't love nobody.

Flashback

Recently reminiscing on possible life positions,
I must say that the thought of you bears fruit that,
Is much sweeter than what could have come to fruition,
For some reason I enjoy wanting you more than I did having you,
I know you belong to someone else now,
I also know that you don't look at him the same way that you look at me,
Do you love him?
Does he make you feel like I do?
Still?
I've realized that it doesn't matter,
I don't bother to ask because I know that you'd lie to me,
Or that you'd lie to yourself,
To keep from realizing the futile progress you've made with someone else,
Ok.
I apologize,
I'm happy for you,
I'm just not happy with myself.

Exit

I wonder if it's too late for you,
Somehow this state of danger seems safe to you,
I see where complacency has taken you,
Absolutely nowhere.
Tell me who's to blame,
Why your life is now like this and things will never be the same,
How it all spiraled out of control and you can no longer maintain,
Tell me if it's too late,
For you to find your way again.

Raincheck

He just doesn't have the time right now,
But he promises you that he's trying,
A forehead kiss coupled with too good to be true words,
I'm not ready to be with you but I want you to be mine,
An array of flags signaling for you to slow your pace,
But somehow to the signs you're blind,
Emotion dominated thoughts cause you to stop using your mind,
Feels like you're losing your mind,
Gave away pieces of yourself to somebody else too many times,
Just to hear the same line,
I'm not ready to be with you but I want you to be mine,
I'll take a rain check,
Please.

Recollection

I loved you before I actually knew what love was
that's how I know I could never consciously do it again.
The way we found ourselves in one another made me believe that roses bloom best- exactly where they belong- between the cracks of concrete.
My eyes filled with tears the moment I realized I'd never feel your touch again.
Reluctant to ever let another in because I'd rather let the pain I've sustained keep me company.
Emotionally speechless wielding a heart shattered to pieces unwilling to let go of the memories eternally begging for time to give you back to me.
Random smiles on rainy days as the recollections play it's all coming back to me now.
Even though I wanted you to stay,
somehow,
it's better this way.

Endless

Silence sustains our safety net as we try not to be constricted by our soul ties,
but neither one of us is bold enough to deny the others presence within our mind.
Parts of me that still belong to you dare to be forgotten and are now constant reminders of how it feels to be surrounded by emptiness.
Even if unpleasant I'm just happy the thought of you is present
and has not decided to subsequently take its leave.
Vibrant words wanting to be said that your ears will never receive become endless love letters written for you that you will never see.
I feel like we still stare at the ceiling at the same time and we roll over in the bed without each other just like we used to.
Random thoughts and unexplainable smiles just as it should be.
I never had the chance to say...
No matter how far you go I just hope you know that I love you.
Endlessly.

Heat of the Moment

How long will our fire burn...
until we learn that lust doesn't last forever.
However, it's not a crime for us to enjoy the time we have left together.
I fall in love every time I fall in you
and both of your lips always reply, saying "I love you too".
I wonder if it's just the heat of the moment
-this feeling that is taking over-
we're willing to accept it but not willing to own it.
How long will our fire burn...
until it's no longer the same, when we're engulfed in one another.
From making love to making up,
once we were both willingly bonded now just feeling stuck.
The spark is gone, and it feels like the fire is fading out.
What did we get ourselves into?
Now we're just trying to make it out,
it's a shame the same fire that kept us together
is the same fire that won't let us out.

Cycle

We love.
even though we know nothing of it
we immerse ourselves within one another
searching for the answers to the questions that we have
embodying enough passion to fuel a thousand lifetimes
we overflow with emotions truly out of our control but still
We hold back.
to what amount will we submit to uncertainty we lose ourselves in the process
I suppose as long as it still feels good
although we both know that we can only hold on for so long
we push ourselves to the brink of insanity just to enjoy the rush
We hurt.
sharing twice as much pain as we do pleasure
we cope with our uneasiness
intensified animosity in our most primitive state
finishing exactly how we started
continuing at the same pace as always
eventually,
We let go.

Sunset

The bright rays embedded with memories now hidden by the clouds of time are desperate to be released from containment,
Your ambience suddenly overwhelms me as my eyes are caught in nature's trance,
Sights of you, sights of what was, and thoughts of what could have been,
If only my dreams would have become reality when it mattered most,
You swear that it's not too late to return to once upon a time
but every beginning must have an end,
And even the sun goes down,
But that doesn't mean it can't rise again.

The Love We Never Made

By the way passion exuded from our pores
and the way our souls surfaced
you'd think these encounters were our sole purpose.
Emotions withheld because only time could tell us
what could possibly happen beyond the inevitable cliffhangers.
A blessing and a curse
what's worse is the fact that our imagination's still have a hold on this moment
even though we wish to own it for ourselves.
Samples to a full-course meal
that could forever satisfy one's soul
has casted undeniable hunger upon me.
I yearn for you.
More than the typical physical connection.
It's a resurrection of a feeling
that was once again felt for the very first time.
A feeling that never belonged to me
that I still feel is mine.
I fell in love...
With the love we never made.

www.ingramcontent.com/pod-product-compliance
Lightning Source LLC
Chambersburg PA
CBHW051709090426
42736CB00013B/2609